PUFFIN BOOKS

Editor: Kaye Webb

Top of the World

'I haven't anything to *do*,' said Donald. It was impossible to keep him happy in their cramped basement flat under the tall office block where their father was caretaker. There wasn't anywhere they were allowed to play, and the moment the children stuck their noses out of the door there was the bossy head porter Mr Hurst telling them off and reminding them that this was no place for children.

'These summer holidays go on far too long,' sighed Mum, but she had to go out shopping, and that made the flat more boring still. 'Kathy, you're in charge,' she said before she went. 'And, Donald, you're to do as Kathy tells you.' Then off she went.

There was only one place Donald wanted to go – the place he called 'heaven'. And the moment Kathy's back was turned, he was on his way. But in his wild and reckless mood, Donald raced headlong into danger, and Kathy faced the most frightening task of her life in rescuing him.

John Rowe Townsend

Top of the World

Illustrated by Nikki Jones

Puffin Books
in association with Oxford University Press

Puffin Books, Penguin Books Ltd, Harmondsworth, Middlesex, England
Penguin Books, 625 Madison Avenue, New York, New York 10022, U.S.A.
Penguin Books Australia Ltd, Ringwood, Victoria, Australia
Penguin Books Canada Ltd, 2801 John Street, Markham, Ontaria, Canada L3R 1B4
Penguin Books (N.Z.) Ltd, 182–190 Wairau Road, Auckland 10, New Zealand

First published by Oxford University Press 1976
Published in Puffin Books 1978

Made and printed in Great Britain by
Hazell Watson & Viney Ltd,
Aylesbury, Bucks
Set in Linotype Juliana

For Penny,
with love

Chapter One

'I want to go to heaven,' Donald said.

'You can't go to heaven today,' said Mum. 'It's Tuesday. Tuesdays I don't go to heaven, I go shopping.'

'I'll go with Dad, then.'

'Not today you won't. It's Dad's day for going to the hospital. He has to have his leg looked at.'

'Well, Kathy can take me.'

'You know very well Kathy can't take you. You don't go to heaven without me or Dad.'

'But I *want* to,' said Donald. 'I haven't anything to *do*.'

Mum sighed. 'I'll be glad when you're back at school, and that's a fact,' she said. 'And I don't suppose you'll be sorry yourself. These summer holidays go on far too long.'

'It's not the holidays,' said Dad. 'It's this place. They don't have anywhere to go but heaven.'

'I could take him,' Kathy said. 'I'd look after him. I wouldn't let him do anything he shouldn't.'

'You'd like to go to heaven too, wouldn't you, Kathy?' said Donald hopefully.

'Not really. But if it would keep you quiet I might.'

Kathy spoke in a superior tone. She was ten and Donald was only seven.

'You are not,' said Mum, 'you are absolutely *not* going there this morning. You can't just go up to heaven whenever you happen to feel like it. And all on your own, too, without any grown-ups.'

Kathy and Donald both knew the way to heaven. It wasn't really called heaven, except by the Barrett family. Its proper name was Top of the World, or simply the Executive Suite.

To get there you had to use the South Elevator. The other two lifts were no good. The other two lifts had twenty buttons, one for each floor of the building, and you pressed the button for whichever floor you wanted to go to. But the South Elevator had twenty-one buttons. The top one didn't have a number on it. Sometimes people pressed it, out of curiosity, but nothing happened. It only worked if you turned a key in the slot at the foot of the panel. And only three or four people had the special key that got you to heaven.

Dad, who was the caretaker at Astral House, had a key. Kathy and Donald had often been up there with him or Mum. You put the key in the slot, turned it to the right, and *then* pressed the twenty-first button. And the elevator soared up, leaving your stomach behind, past floor after floor, taking no notice of anybody who might be waiting. It passed, last of all, the staff cafeteria on the twentieth floor. It stopped at roof level. You got out of it there and walked along a corridor that ended in an archway. Beyond the archway you could see a garden, out in the open air. To your right, just inside the archway, was a door – a handsome door of natural wood. Above the door was a beautifully lettered sign, TOP OF THE WORLD. And across the foot of the sign, in smaller letters, in case anybody didn't know what that meant, were the words 'Astral Assurance Company Executive Suite'.

That was where important people visiting the company stayed. The company was very proud of the Executive Suite. It thought visitors were much more comfortable there than if they stayed at one of the big hotels. And so they were. Kathy's and Donald's mum kept the Executive Suite all spick and span. That was her job. The suite was dusted every day, and thoroughly cleaned once a week, whether anybody had stayed in it or not.

The Executive Suite was a big, beautiful, rooftop flat. And the nicest thing about it was the garden. When you first glimpsed it, through that archway, it was almost too pretty to be true. Most of it was paved, but there was a neat little lawn, bright and green and carefully trimmed, and in the middle of it a fountain and a goldfish pond. And there were trees in tubs, and flower-beds, and hanging-baskets that were changed with the season, and white ironwork seats, and a tiny summer-house. And everything was taken care of by Dad.

The garden was at the south end of the roof, so it got all the sun. To the north the garden was protected by a wall, which was actually the side of an even higher stretch of flat roof. And the east and west edges of the garden had sheltering walls to keep out the wind. But the south end had only a balustrade. Grown-ups could lean on it and enjoy the view. It looked out across the southern part of the city, and beyond it the country-side, and in the distance, miles and miles away, the violet-grey hills. And between those hills, on a clear day, you could see the sea.

The first time Dad had taken the children up there, soon after he got the job at Astral House a year ago, Donald had looked around wide-eyed and asked, 'Is it heaven?' And since then the Executive Suite and

garden had always been known to the Barretts as heaven. 'If this is heaven, I wonder what we should call our own flat, down in the basement,' Dad would say sometimes, but Mum always hushed him. 'It's a *nice* flat,' she'd say, 'all things considered.'

'Well, you two,' Dad said to the children now, 'you'll just have to play quietly while your mum and I are away.'

'I suppose I *could* shop some other time,' Mum said. 'But I do like to get it done Tuesday morning, and there's so much we need. And I don't see what harm the children can come to. And Kathy's *very* responsible, aren't you, dear?'

Kathy didn't say anything but she was pleased. She liked it when Mum or Dad made a remark like that. It made her feel grown-up.

Donald wasn't so pleased. He was in a grouchy mood that morning.

'I wish there was someone *else* to play with,' he said. 'Kathy doesn't play properly. Always reading or something.' And he went on, in a complaining tone of voice, 'Nowhere to go, nothing to do. And old Mr Hurst shouting at me as soon's I put my head out of the door.'

'This morning you're not to *put* your head out of the door,' Mum told him sharply. Then she sighed.

'I know it's not ideal for children,' she said. 'Here in a city centre with all the traffic around and nobody to

play with. But I suppose we should be thankful your dad has a job at all, with his disability. And at least it gives us somewhere to live. As for Mr Hurst . . .'

'Don't you go offending Mr Hurst!' Dad said. 'And don't give him any cheek. Remember who he is.'

Mum sighed again. Mr Hurst was the head porter – or rather, since last month, he was the Building Supervisor. That was a new title for the same job, but it made Mr Hurst feel more important. And it seemed to the Barretts that Mr Hurst felt important enough already.

Mr Hurst was big and bossy. And everybody knew that if he'd had his way Dad wouldn't have got his job as caretaker. Mr Hurst thought it was a job for a childless person. He thought it was a job for an able-bodied person, too, and Dad wasn't quite able-bodied. Dad had a permanent limp, the result of a wound he'd got in Northern Ireland, and it still played him up sometimes.

'He'd have us out in the street if he could,' Dad said.

Kathy had a sudden horrid vision of them all huddled together on the pavement outside Astral House, surrounded by their furniture. And in pouring rain, probably . . .

'There, that's enough, you'll frighten the children,' Mum told Dad. 'And don't worry, you know Mr Hurst can't sack anybody. Only the Staff Manager can do that, and I don't see why he should sack *you*. You do your work well. That garden's a joy to behold.'

'Mr Hurst doesn't care about the garden,' Dad said. 'And he does have the Staff Manager's ear. There's no telling what he says to him. Every time one of us puts a foot wrong, I start getting worried.'

'Oh, stop it, Len, do. It's having to go to the hospital that's making you so gloomy. You're cheerful enough as a rule.'

That was true. Dad was usually in good spirits. He was small, willing, easygoing, and eager to please. Mum was taller than Dad, and tougher. What Mum said, went.

'Well, it's high time we were away,' Mum said. 'Remember, Kathy, you're in charge. And Donald, you're to do as Kathy tells you.'

Donald mouthed some words that nobody could hear.

'Mum, he was saying something rude, I know he was,' said Kathy.

'I wasn't!' said Donald indignantly. 'At least, not about you. It was about Mr Hurst.'

'And what did you say about Mr Hurst?' demanded Dad.

'I said he's fat and stupid, that's all.'

'Sometimes he calls Mr Hurst "Dirty Bertie",' said Kathy.

Mum and Dad both tried to look cross, but they caught each other's eyes and couldn't quite prevent themselves from smiling.

'Well, Mr Hurst certainly isn't dirty,' said Mum. 'I

won't comment on the "fat and stupid". Except to say that you are *not* to be rude about him, whatever you think. And just you keep out of his way!'

Chapter Two

Donald was still grumbling.

'Can't go out in the street, can't play in the building, can't go up on the roof, can't do *anything*.'

'Oh, stop complaining, Donald,' said Kathy, in a voice that was meant to sound like her mother's. 'Just you play quietly on the floor while I wash these dishes.'

'I'll dry the dishes for you,' Donald offered.

'Oh, no, you won't,' said Kathy. '*I'll* dry the dishes. You'd only break them.'

'I was being nice!' said Donald, outraged. It looked for a moment as if he was going to make a fuss. But there was no one he could make a fuss *to*, so he thought better of it. He got out his collection of toy cars. In a minute or two, Kathy could hear him making brum-brum noises on the sitting-room carpet.

'Well, that takes care of *him*,' Kathy said aloud, in the tones of one grown-up talking to another. But actually she felt much the same as Donald did. It wasn't much fun being cooped up in this basement flat, with no other children to play with. And when the

sun shone, as it was doing today, she wanted to be out of doors. But there wasn't any out of doors where they could be. Except, of course, heaven. And they couldn't go to heaven on their own.

She was drying the last of the dishes when the doorbell rang. Kathy answered it, and had an instant feeling of alarm in her stomach. Mr Hurst loomed bulkily in the doorway.

Mr Hurst had a beefy red face and a big bushy grey moustache. His hair was grey, too, but there wasn't much of it, and it was carefully combed so as to cover as much of his scalp as possible. He was twice as big as Dad, and his black military-style uniform looked as

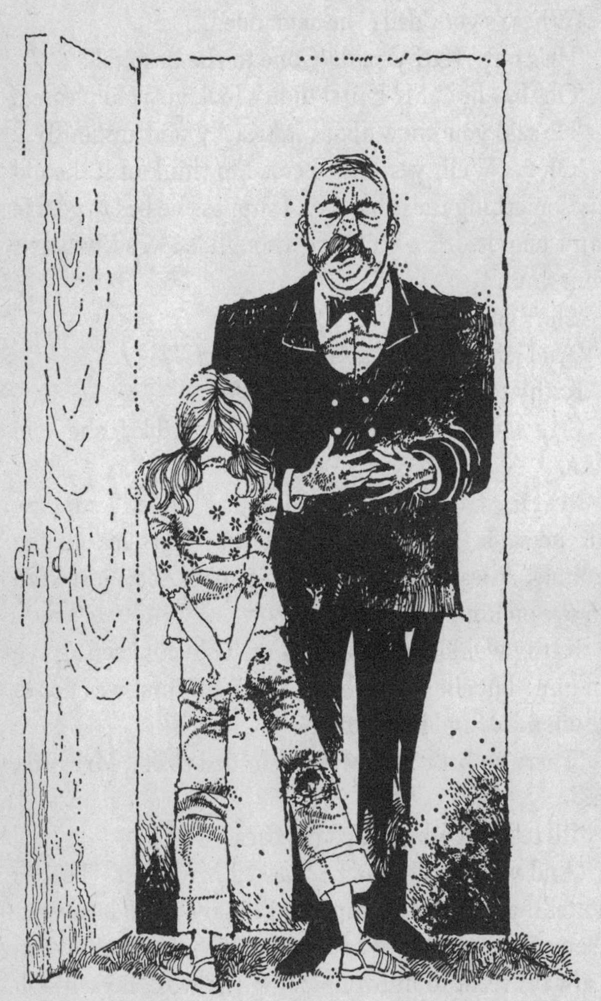

if it had a struggle to meet round his midriff. There were three gold stripes on his arm.

'Where's your dad?' he demanded.

'He's out,' Kathy said. 'Gone to the hospital.'

'Oh, *has* he?' Mr Hurst didn't look any too pleased.

'He said you knew about it,' Kathy said anxiously.

'Oh ... Well, yes, now I come to think of it, he did say something the other day. I suppose he has to go. He can't help it. It's a nuisance, though ... Well, where's your mum?'

'She's gone shopping.'

'And left you two kids on your own?'

Kathy tossed her head just a little.

'My mother says I'm very responsible,' she told him.

Mr Hurst looked at her without a smile. 'I suppose so,' he said. 'It's the other one that gives me all the trouble. Always up to something, he is. You just keep an eye on him.'

Kathy would have liked to say, 'I *always* keep an eye on him,' but she remembered that Mr Hurst was not to be offended, and kept quiet.

'There's a little job I want your dad to do,' Mr Hurst said.

'I'll tell him when he comes back.'

'And when will that be?' asked Mr Hurst. 'There's no telling, is there? I suppose I'll have to do it myself. I sometimes wonder what good it is having staff, when I always seem to finish up doing the work myself. Oh well, such is life. Now I'll need to borrow a spanner. Do you know where your dad keeps his tools?'

Kathy did know. She took Mr Hurst through the kitchen to the scullery and opened the battered chest of drawers where Dad's tools were. Mr Hurst rummaged among them while she stood by. After a minute or two he came up with two or three spanners of different sizes.

'One of these should do the trick,' he said. 'I hope. If your dad comes back, tell him I've taken them. Though I'll probably be back here before he is. He might be all morning at that hospital.'

Kathy let him out of the flat. She was glad when he'd gone. There was something about Mr Hurst that made her feel as if she might be in trouble any minute without knowing what she was in trouble about. She began putting the dishes away. After a minute she remembered Donald, and called out,

'I'll play a game with you when I've finished. What would you like to play?'

There was no answer from the sitting-room.

'Donald!' Kathy called crossly.

Still no reply.

Kathy was suddenly anxious. She hurried into the next room. Donald's toy cars were still on the carpet, but Donald wasn't.

She pushed open the bathroom door. No Donald.

'Donald! Donald!' As she was shouting, Kathy dashed through the remaining rooms of the flat. And there was no doubt about it. Donald was gone. He must have let himself out while she was in the kitchen talking to Mr Hurst.

'Oh, Donald, *Donald*!' Kathy half shrieked, half wailed his name as she ran up the steps from the basement to the main lobby of Astral House.

Chapter Three

In the entrance to the building, Mr Hurst, with the spanners still in his hand, was talking to the porter, Mr Jones. People kept coming in and out, and Mr Hurst and Mr Jones broke off every few seconds to say 'Good morning' to somebody they knew. They were so used to doing this that they could carry on a conversation without even noticing the interruptions.

Kathy ran up to them, breathless. Mr Hurst looked her up and down. He didn't like seeing children around the building. He thought they made the place untidy.

'Well?' he said shortly.

'It's Donald!'

'Donald? Oh, your brother. *That* kid. What's he been doing now?'

'He's gone!'

Mr Hurst was never very quick on the uptake.

'Gone where?' he asked.

'I don't know where. He was in the flat a minute or two ago when you came in, but now he isn't. He must have slipped out while we were looking for the spanners.'

'He would,' said Mr Hurst.

'Well, I can tell you this,' said Mr Jones. 'He hasn't gone out of the building. I've been here in this doorway all the time, and I keep my eyes open. I'd have seen him.'

'Then he's on the premises somewhere!' said Mr Hurst. 'And running around the corridors, getting under people's feet, I expect. I've had more than enough of that boy, I can tell you. If he gets up to any more mischief, I'll . . .'

Mr Hurst broke off suddenly.

'Reg! Look!' he said to Mr Jones. And both men turned away from Kathy, seeming to forget all about her.

A long black car had pulled up outside the building. A chauffeur was holding its back door open. And out of it, very slowly, came a little old man with a beaky nose and thick white hair. The chauffeur made as if to help him on with his coat, but the old man waved him away. Then, slowly and carefully but without stumbling, he climbed the steps, entered the building, and walked across the shiny black-tiled floor of the lobby towards the lifts.

'Mr Jones! Attention!' snapped Mr Hurst. He clicked his heels together and gave a smart military salute. Mr Jones came to attention too, rather sloppily. He looked embarrassed.

'Good morning, sir!' said Mr Hurst, loudly.

''Morning, Hurst!' the old man said. He added mildly, in a quiet voice, 'You don't have to do that, you know.'

Mr Jones winked slyly at Kathy. Kathy was still worrying about Donald and wondering what she should do. To Mr Hurst this little old man was obviously much more important than a missing small boy.

'The South Elevator, sir?' Mr Hurst asked in a very efficient tone of voice; and in response to a nod, he walked ahead of the old man and flung the gate of the lift open with a flourish.

'Who is he?' whispered Kathy to Mr Jones.

'Don't you know? That's the President.'

'The President of the United States?' asked Kathy, round-eyed.

Mr Jones laughed.

'No, no. The President of Astral Assurance.'

'Oh,' said Kathy blankly.

'He's the top man of all. You know they have an even bigger building than this in London. And offices all over the world. And thousands of people working for them. Well, he's Number One. Mr Swanson, that's who he is. He doesn't come here often, now he's getting on in years. But he's sharp, you know. He doesn't forget anything. Did you notice, he remembered Hursty's name all right, though I bet he hasn't seen him for months.'

Mr Hurst was coming back to them from the lift.

'He went up by himself,' he told them. 'Wouldn't

let me take him. "I'm not helpless, Hurst," he says. "I still have the strength to press a button," he says. What do you make of that, Reg?'

'Well, I suppose he *has* the strength to press a button,' Mr Jones said. 'Where's he gone, Bert? His own office? I hope they've got it ready for him. It's a long time since he was here last.'

'No, he's gone straight up to Top of the World,' said Mr Hurst. 'I don't think anyone expected him today. It's a surprise visit. And he wants lunch served up there, for him and a guest. I'd better warn the Catering Manager. They'll want to get busy on something special. He's fussy about his food ...' Mr Hurst's eyes fell on Kathy.

'*You* still here,' he said. 'What was it you wanted?'

'It's *Donald*,' said Kathy. Suddenly she was almost in tears. 'What's happened to him? What will my mum say?'

'There, there,' said Mr Jones. 'Don't worry love, I told you, he hasn't gone out of the building. He can't have come to any harm.'

'Mr Jones and I,' said Mr Hurst in an important tone, 'will go and look for your brother as soon as I've arranged for the President's lunch. The front door can take care of itself for a few minutes.' He finished in a more normal voice: 'And when I catch that little blighter, he'll know about it!'

They went off, with Mr Hurst still holding Dad's spanners. Kathy looked after them. Her eyes were still prickling with tears. She'd been left in charge of Donald, and there'd been disaster almost at once. She didn't know which worried her more – what had become of Donald, or what Mum was going to say if he was still missing. And she didn't dare think about Dad. What if she and Donald between them lost Dad his job?

On the desk in the lobby, the telephone rang.

Kathy looked at it nervously. She wasn't very good at the telephone. If people asked her things she didn't know about, she usually got tongue-tied and frightened. She hoped it would stop ringing. But it didn't. It rang and rang.

Kathy went up to the desk. There was a chair where the porter on duty sometimes sat, though more often he'd be standing in the doorway.

No sign of Mr Hurst or Mr Jones.

Reluctantly she took the telephone off the hook.

'Hello,' she said. And then, remembering the words the porters always used, she added, 'Reception Desk.'

She knew at once whose voice it was. A thin, precise voice. An old man's voice that managed to keep steady, without a waver to it. Mr Swanson. The President. He spoke the way he'd come up those steps – slowly and carefully.

'Is Hurst there at present?' he asked.

'N-no.'

'Or the other man? Jones?'

'No.'

'What's happened to them?'

'I – I don't know. I think they'll be back soon.'

'Good. Well, as soon as one of them appears, tell him to come straight up to Top of the World, will you? There's –' Mr Swanson paused as if he could hardly believe what he was saying, then went on: 'There's a *child* in the garden up here. A little boy. He is . . .' Mr Swanson paused again. 'He is bathing in the fountain.'

'Oh!' said Kathy. She drew in breath sharply. 'It's Donald.'

'It's what?'

'It's Donald,' Kathy said in a very small voice.

'Whatever it is,' said Mr Swanson, 'I should like it removed.'

Chapter Four

'Donald's my brother,' Kathy said. 'I'll come up and fetch him.'

'That would be rather a good idea,' said Mr Swanson. 'I think perhaps you should bring a towel. He looks extremely wet. Extraordinary ... No, on second thoughts I don't think you need bring a towel after all. There's a line of *washing* hanging out here, and several towels on it.'

'Oh, goodness!' Kathy said. 'That's Mum's. She does hang the washing out there, when visitors aren't expected. There isn't anywhere else to put a clothes line.'

'*Most* extraordinary!' said Mr Swanson.

'I'll come right away,' Kathy promised.

She put down the receiver and hurried back to the basement flat, intending to climb on a chair and get the special elevator key from where it was kept on a high shelf. The place was supposed to be secret, but she and Donald both knew about it. And when she got to the room where it was, she saw that a chair had been moved across already and was standing just under the shelf.

Of course! Donald had been there before her. The key was gone.

Without the special key, the South Elevator was no better than the other two. They would all take you to the twentieth floor and no farther. Kathy didn't know how you got from the twentieth floor to the roof, or even whether you *could*. But she would have to try. She ran back to the lobby, heading for the nearest lift. Mr Hurst and Mr Jones were still away.

Then a thought struck her. She went across to the reception desk and opened the top right-hand drawer. There, as she'd remembered, was a whole bunch of keys. And one of them, she knew, was the special key for the South Elevator.

At any other time, Kathy wouldn't have dreamed of taking the keys. But this time the need was desper-

ate. She hardly thought about it. She grabbed the whole bunch, ran to the South Elevator, and pressed the call button.

The elevator wasn't in place. It was up at the sixteenth floor. A light that shone from behind a row of numerals, and at present was picking out the number 16, told her that. She jabbed her finger on the call button again and again, though she knew it didn't make any difference. It seemed an age before the light started moving down the row of numerals, showing that the lift was coming. 15, the indicator said, then 14, 13, 12, 11 ... It came down quickly until it reached Number 8, and then it stuck. Somebody must be getting in or out, and taking plenty of time over it.

As the indicator stayed on and on at Number 8, Kathy felt a rapidly rising panic. There was no telling what Donald might be up to by now, and here she was, helpless. Perhaps the lift had gone wrong, and wouldn't come down to the lobby at all. Number 8, it was still saying, 8, 8, 8, 8, 8. She wanted to bite her nails, but that was a habit she'd broken ...

Then the lift was moving again. It couldn't have stopped for more than a few seconds, but they'd been the longest seconds of her life. 7, 6, 5 showed on the indicator, then 4, 3, 2, 1, and here it was. Two or three people got out. Kathy got in. Then she was fumbling with the big heavy bunch of keys, trying the ones that looked the right size.

The first two she tried were wrong, and wouldn't go

in the slot. The third key was the right one and went in, but at first she couldn't turn it. Kathy felt renewed flutterings of panic in her stomach. At any moment somebody might step into the lift and ask her what she was doing with all those keys.

She didn't quite know how it happened, but suddenly, as she fiddled, the key turned. She pressed the top button, the gate clanged shut, and the elevator was soaring towards the roof.

Kathy had a strange feeling in her throat, as though she'd have cried if she hadn't been too busy. Donald was up there, and a line of washing, too. And Mr Swanson was the very top man of all. Number One, Mr Jones had called him. And if Mr Hurst found the Barrett family a nuisance, what was somebody as important as Mr Swanson going to think? Perhaps he'd just say 'I'd like them removed,' the way he'd said it about Donald a minute or two ago. And they'd all be thrown out into the street. She had that horrid vision again of the whole family with their furniture around them, out there on the pavement in the pouring rain. It wouldn't be like that *really*, she knew, but still . . .

The elevator stopped at the top. Kathy got out and hurried along the corridor. The beautiful door of the Executive Suite was shut. But Mr Swanson was standing in the archway that led to the garden. At his back, the sunshine was blindingly bright.

'Ah, there you are,' Mr Swanson said. 'I'm so glad

you've come. I've been wondering what that boy would do next. And perhaps I'd rather not find out. Just look at him now.'

Donald was kneeling on the edge of the goldfish pond, leaning perilously forward with cupped hands. Beside him was a red plastic bowl that Mum used when she washed dishes in the Executive Suite.

And – what seemed to Kathy the most shocking thing of all – he was naked. His shorts and tee-shirt lay where he'd dropped them on the way to the fountain.

Kathy shot a startled glance at Mr Swanson. Donald's nakedness didn't seem to be bothering him, but he had a somewhat helpless air, as if he'd arrived on a scene that was outside his experience, and didn't know what to do.

'He's caught a goldfish already,' he told Kathy in a tone of wonder, 'and put it in that bowl.'

'Donald!' Kathy shouted. 'You naughty boy! Come out at once, and get some clothes on!'

Donald stopped fishing long enough to wave.

'Hello, Kathy!' he called cheerfully.

'I told you, come out!'

Donald never heard what he didn't want to hear. He cupped his hands together and dipped them in the water again, taking no notice. Kathy ran towards him. But Donald had been expecting this. He was as quick and slippery as a fish himself. She got her hands to his wet body, but he slithered out of her grip and raced away.

And in a moment he was on the ladder that led from the garden to the higher part of the roof.

Chapter Five

Kathy gasped, with real dismay. It oughtn't to have been possible for Donald to get on to that ladder. Normally, when it wasn't in use, its lower part slid up behind its top half, and it was too high for a child to reach. Getting it down into position required a strong adult pull on a handle. That was a safety precaution. Astral Assurance was careful about safety precautions.

But the precaution had come unstuck. The ladder was ready for use. Some workmen had left it like that, perhaps. Or even – could it be that Mum or Dad was to blame? That possibility was too awful. But Kathy didn't have time to think about it. For here was the ladder, reaching from the garden to the main roof above; and here was Donald. Or rather, here wasn't Donald. He was up the ladder, over the top, and out of sight in a matter of seconds.

'Donald! Donald!' Kathy shrieked.

Mr Swanson sat down heavily on the garden seat. His face was pale. He looked old, tired and alarmed.

'Donald! Where are you? Come back!' Kathy was still shrieking.

Donald reappeared at the edge above, and looked down at them both.

'Hey, Kathy, it's great up here!' he called.

'Donald! You know you mustn't be up there. It isn't safe!'

'It's all right. A bit windy, though.'

'Come down at once!'

'I won't!'

'You must!'

'Who says so?'

Mr Swanson got up, with an effort, from the seat.

'Donald,' he called. 'I say so. You must come down at once.'

'Who's he?' Donald asked Kathy.

'He's Mr Swanson. He's the President.'

'What's a President?'

'He's the boss. The boss of the whole company.'

'Is he boss over Dad?'

'Yes.'

'Is he boss over *Mr Hurst*?'

'Yes, he is. He's boss over all the people who work in this building. Every one. So do as you're told. Come down quickly. And get some clothes on, you're disgusting.'

It seemed for a moment as if Donald would come down. He looked at Mr Swanson with respect. Then a thought struck him, and his face lit up with triumph.

'He's not boss over *me*,' he said. 'Because I don't work for the company. I'm not big enough.'

'Oh, *Donald*!' Kathy was in despair. 'Listen, I told you, he's boss over Dad, and Dad's boss over you, so *of course* he's boss over you, so come down this minute!'

'Donald, *please* come down,' said Mr Swanson. The elderly voice was quiet but steady. Kathy felt the force of command. Probably anybody in the building would have done what Mr Swanson said when he spoke in that tone of voice. Anybody *else* in the building, that is. But it didn't work on Donald.

'No, thank you,' he said. 'I like it here. I'm staying.'

Kathy said desperately to Mr Swanson, 'I'll have to go up there. It's the only way I'll get him down.'

'No, no, child,' Mr Swanson said. 'I shall telephone

downstairs again. This is a job for Hurst and the porters. You keep him talking until they come.'

He had spoken quietly, but Donald heard part of what he said.

'If anyone else comes,' he told Kathy as Mr Swanson walked back towards the Executive Suite, 'I'll just run away across the roof. I bet they can't catch me. I bet *nobody* can catch me.'

'Oh, Donald, we'll be in such *trouble*!' Kathy said miserably.

But Donald was excited and triumphant. Kathy knew just what mood he'd be in by now. He'd be getting above himself. He'd be in a state that Mum called 'silly-giddy', when he might say or do anything.

'Don't care!' he proclaimed. 'Don't care!'

'I'm coming up,' Kathy said with quiet determination. 'And I'm bringing your clothes. You can put them on before you come down here. What will people think if they see you running around like that?'

'Don't care, don't care!' repeated Donald. 'And I bet you daren't come up. You'll be frightened. It's windy up here, and there's no wall round this part of the roof. You'll be afraid of being blown off the edge.'

'But Donald!' Kathy almost wept. 'What if *you're* blown off the edge?'

Chapter Six

Kathy hadn't any head for heights. Even the metal ladder that went up twelve feet or so from the Executive Suite garden to the main rooftop was enough to make her feel dizzy. She tucked Donald's shorts and tee-shirt into the top of her jeans, to keep her hands free. Then she gripped the sides of the ladder until they nearly cut into her flesh, and placed each foot with enormous care as she climbed. She didn't dare to look down. At the top, the sides of the ladder extended above the level of the roof. Kathy stepped hastily through on to firm ground, and didn't turn round until she was well away from the edge.

The roof was flat and concreted, and it stretched a long way. Kathy hadn't realized the building was so large. And although the late summer sun was quite warm, it felt bleak up here. A steady breeze swept across the bare concrete. It was a bit like a seaside promenade out of season, or even like a deserted beach, except that it was up in the sky. It felt like the edge of things. It didn't feel like the kind of place where people could walk and talk easily, and be comfortable together.

Donald seemed to be quite at home, though. He spoke to her as if she'd come up to play with him.

'It's good up here, isn't it?' he said. 'We could have all kinds of games. We could play tag. Or if we had a ball, we could throw catches.'

Kathy shuddered, imagining a ball being blown by the wind, imagining Donald chasing it towards the roof's edge. He'd be watching the ball, not watching where he was going ... For a moment the ground beneath her seemed to tilt sideways. Then it righted itself.

'Are you all right, Kathy?' Donald asked.

'Yes, I'm all right.'

'I can see the Resident.'

'The President.' Kathy corrected him automatically.

She swallowed, turned, and looked back into the roof garden, a little way below them. Suddenly it seemed secure and friendly, with its neat little lawn and its seats and fountain, and its trees in tubs and its safely-walled sides.

You could see from here that the Executive Suite was a kind of bungalow. And you could indeed see the President, through one of its windows. He was telephoning.

And beyond the Executive Suite there was space, and the tops of two or three other tall buildings, and a church spire, and a clock tower. Birds flew below your eye level. You couldn't see the nearest streets from this angle, but you could see the railway station, and a train crawling along the tracks, looking like a caterpillar.

And you could see a canal, and a river, and parks, and miles of red-brick housing. And beyond that, country and hills and sea. And if you looked all about you, the entire view made one enormous circle, as if to prove that the world was really and truly round.

Kathy shuddered again. It was fascinating, but it frightened her.

'What shall we do first?' Donald asked.

'Donald, we have to go *down*. Don't you understand? We're not supposed to *be* here.'

But Donald, once again, seemed not to hear what she said; at any rate, he took no notice.

'We could go and explore,' he suggested.

Kathy moved rapidly towards him and grabbed his arm. Donald struggled. She held on firmly. He tried to jerk himself away, but couldn't break her grip. Then he hit her with his free hand. That hurt, but the pain was not as strong as Kathy's urge to hold him. She got both arms round him, and clung to him in a bear-hug.

Then Mr Swanson came out of the Executive Suite. In his slow and careful way, he was *running*.

'Donald! Don't struggle!' he called. But Donald only struggled more.

Mr Swanson came towards the ladder. When he reached the foot of it he was out of Kathy's sight, but soon there were scraping sounds as he clambered slowly upwards. Kathy could hear his laboured breathing. It was a long time before his head came into view. She hung on grimly, hoping that Donald would tire.

But as Mr Swanson reached the top of the ladder, Donald had a fresh surge of energy. He couldn't get away from Kathy, but he pushed her back towards the edge, so that if they'd moved another foot or two they'd have toppled into the roof garden. Kathy, terrified, loosened her grip at last. Donald broke away from her and drew back to a safe distance.

Then he started grinning.

'Yah! Can't catch me!' he jeered. He advanced a few feet, tempting her to chase him, but she didn't move.

Mr Swanson had stepped off the ladder now, and stood beside Kathy. He was still breathing hard. He looked exhausted and distressed.

'I'm sorry I let him go,' Kathy said.

'You couldn't help it, my dear.'

'If only I could have held on just a bit longer, till you came.'

'I'm not sure that even the two of us together could have held him,' said Mr Swanson.

'Is Mr Hurst coming?'

'I hope so. I spoke to him on the phone just now. He says Jones isn't there and the keys have disappeared from the reception desk.'

Kathy felt suddenly guilty, and blushed, but Mr Swanson didn't seem to notice.

'However,' he went on, 'Hurst can get other keys. He'll be here as soon as possible.'

Mr Swanson sighed.

'I think Hurst understood the urgency of it,' he said. 'But oh, my goodness, it's a worry.'

Donald's success in getting away from Kathy had gone to his head. His mood now was sillier and giddier than ever.

'Can't catch me!' he taunted them again.

'I think we'd better not try,' Mr Swanson said quietly to Kathy. 'He's safer where he is than being chased all over the roof. We'll wait here until help comes.'

'Yoo-hoo, silly old Kathy, can't catch me!' Donald jeered.

'I don't want to!' Kathy told him. 'You'll be in trouble now, and it's your own fault. You'll be in *great big* trouble. Mr Hurst's coming!'

That made Donald stop and think. He was much more afraid of Mr Hurst than of the President. But it was only for a second. He was in a state in which it didn't matter how much trouble he got into later on, the excitement of the moment was worth it.

'I'm going to the edge!' he declared.

Kathy couldn't pretend not to care about that.

'Donald, *don't*! There's no wall or fence or *anything*! And this wind! You'll fall off.'

'I won't. I'm going to *spit* right down into the street.'

And Donald ran across the open roof to the edge, two hundred feet above the street below. The wind was enough to lift his hair. His naked body looked very small and frail – light enough, almost, to be blown away.

Kathy moved to follow him, but Mr Swanson caught her arm. There were tiny beads of sweat along the lines in his forehead.

'No,' he said, 'If you went after him now, he'd be *more* likely to go over.'

Donald stood within a foot or so of the edge. Then he looked around to see what reaction he was getting from Mr Swanson and Kathy. They stood still, trying not to show any signs of alarm. Donald moved an inch or two closer to the edge, glanced around again, and leaned slowly forward, looking over.

'There's a crane over there!' he called. 'Working on another building. I'm going to wave to the man!'

Then a shiver moved across his body. He stepped back from the edge, hugged himself briefly, and shivered again. And he walked towards Kathy, stopping at a safe distance.

'You're getting cold, aren't you?' Kathy said. 'Serve you right!'

'Give me my clothes, Kathy!'

'I will if you promise to come straight down.'

'Give me my clothes!'

'No!'

'Meany! Meany! Give me them!'

'Not till you promise.'

'I'll do something worse if you don't give me them. I'll sit on the edge.'

'Oh, Donald, no!'

'I will, I will!'

'He would, too,' Kathy said helplessly.

'I think I should give him his clothes,' Mr Swanson said. And then, 'I wish Hurst would show up. He ought to be here by now.'

'*Can* Mr Hurst get him down?' Kathy asked miserably. 'Can *anyone*?'

'If Hurst puts on his best sergeant-major act, it might just make the boy do as he's told. If not... well, we'll have to think about the next move. It could be that we'd do best to go inside the Suite and leave him to get bored and come down of his own accord. But I don't like doing that, do you?'

'No,' said Kathy. Then she had a bright idea. 'If I give you your clothes, Donald,' she called, 'will you promise not to go to the edge again?'

Donald hesitated. Then he shivered once more.

'All right,' he said. He approached her warily. 'Throw me them.'

Mr Swanson nodded. Kathy threw the clothes. Donald darted in and picked them up. Then he drew back to a safe distance and put them on.

'Well, at least he looks more respectable,' Kathy said, though even as she said it, it struck her that that was not the tiniest bit important.

Donald moved farther away.

'Remember what you promised!' Kathy reminded him.

'All right, I won't go to the edge,' Donald said. 'I'm going up there instead.'

'Oh, my God!' said Mr Swanson.

Donald was pointing to the other side of the roof, where a small square structure rose ten feet or so above the main surface. A metal ladder, smaller and frailer than the one that led from the roof garden, clung to its side. On top of it were a flagstaff and a few aerials. It was the highest point of the whole building.

'What is it?' Kathy asked.

'It's above the elevators. It holds the winding gear, I suppose. I don't know much about these things. And it has the big electric sign on the side that faces outwards. The Astral Assurance sign, the two As. You can see it from twenty miles away, they say, on a clear night.'

'I'm going up that ladder!' Donald declared. 'I promised not to go to the edge. I didn't promise not to go up a ladder. When I'm up there I'll be really at the top. The top of the top of the top!'

Chapter Seven

Kathy and Mr Swanson walked slowly across the flat roof towards the raised section. A shadow moved over the roof as a fleck of cloud crossed the sun. The wind blew steadily, and a seagull slid past in a long curving flight, its spread wings unmoving. Donald danced and jumped ahead of them. He enjoyed letting them come close, then darting away, knowing they couldn't catch him.

'I can climb it one-handed!' he shouted as he went up the last frail ladder. Then he was looking down on them from the top.

'I'm the king of the castle!' he chanted. '*I'm* the king of the castle!'

That was the moment when Mr Hurst arrived on the scene. He ran heavily, clumsily towards them. He saw and heard Donald. And he reacted exactly as Kathy would have expected him to react.

'Come down from there *at* once!' he roared.

Donald was suddenly still and silent.

Mr Hurst, solid as a bull, with beefy face and bushy moustache, and the three gold stripes on his arm, was the most powerful figure Donald had ever known, the only person he'd ever feared.

'Come on! Down you come! Now!'

Mr Hurst pointed to the foot of the ladder.

Slowly, as if hypnotized, Donald approached the top of it. He put a foot on it, then another foot, then took a step down, and another step. He took a third step down, more hesitantly. Mr Hurst came to the bottom of the ladder and stretched his arms up, meaning to grab Donald the moment he was in reach. This was a mistake. Donald started away and went back up a step.

'Mr Hurst won't hurt you,' Mr Swanson said quietly. 'Nobody's going to hurt you.'

But Donald was at the top of the ladder again. He stepped off it and looked down at them doubtfully.

'If I have to come up for you ...' Mr Hurst threatened. He was so cross that he didn't realize he was making Donald disbelieve Mr Swanson. He put both hands on the sides of the ladder and a foot on the lowest rung, ready to climb.

Kathy gave a little moan. She couldn't help it. She was imagining Mr Hurst up there, trying to grab Donald, and Donald dancing away, back to the edge, perhaps. There just wasn't *room* for a skirmish in that small amount of space.

'Come back, Hurst,' Mr Swanson said, in that quiet tone of authority he'd used once before. Reluctantly Mr Hurst stepped away from the ladder. But he still thought he could bring Donald down by force of will.

'For the last time,' he called; and then, in a sergeant-major's bellow, with a podgy finger pointing to the ground in front of him, 'DOWN ! ! !'

Once more it almost worked. Donald came to the top of the ladder again and seemed about to descend it. And then – Kathy never knew why it was, but perhaps it was because for once he was higher up than Mr Hurst, looking down on his bald patch instead of up to his impressive midriff – Donald's mood changed, and he was wilder than ever.

'Get lost, Bertie Hurst !' he yelled down. 'Bertie, Bertie, Bertie, can't catch me !' He did a little dance at the top of the ladder and shouted,

'I'm the king of the castle,
Get down you dirty rascal !

Dirty Bertie, Dirty Bertie, Dirty Bertie !'

And then in his turn Mr Hurst went wild. His temper snapped.

'I've had enough from you, Donald Barrett !' he bawled. 'I'll beat the daylights out of you !' And he went charging up the ladder.

'No, Hurst, no !' Mr Swanson begged him. But it was in vain. He was at the top, and Donald was darting away from him, out of sight from below. Then Mr Hurst was shouting something to Donald in quite a different voice, alarmed instead of angry. And a moment later Mr Hurst reappeared at the top of the ladder, shaken.

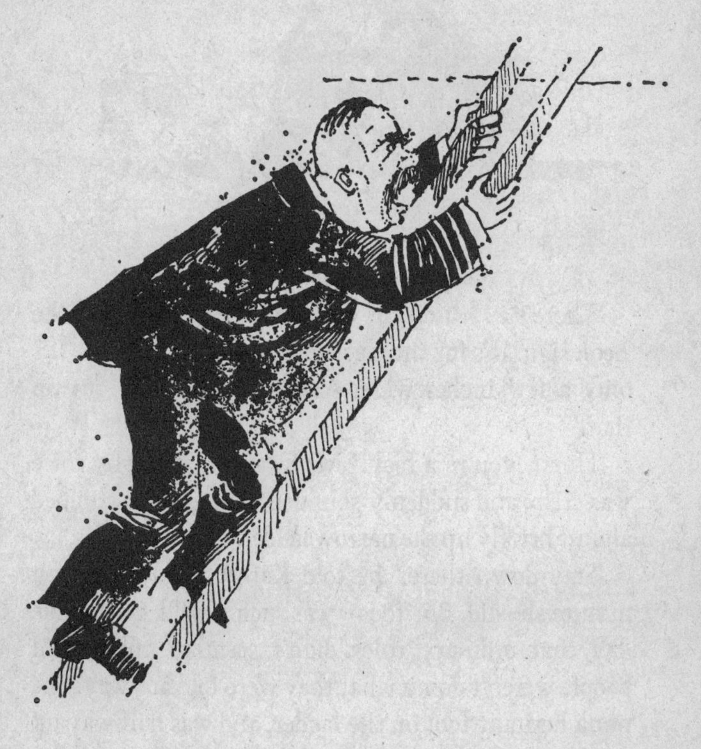

'There's a . . . a sort of walkway,' he said. 'Under the neon sign. It's for the electricians.' He swallowed. 'It's only a few inches wide. And Donald's gone out on that.'

'Hurst, you're a fool!' Mr Swanson said. His voice was crisp, and suddenly sounded younger. He climbed almost briskly up the narrow ladder.

'Stay down there,' he told Kathy. And for half a minute she did. But today was such a wild, impossible day that ordinary rules didn't seem to apply, and people weren't doing what they were told anyway. She put a hesitant foot on the ladder, and was half way up it when Mr Swanson reappeared.

'Kathy,' he said, 'I think you'd better come after all. You may be needed. But take care. Take great care.'

Gingerly, Kathy mounted to the top. This highest section of roof was about the size of a large living-room. In a way it was safer than the main roof area. At the side which dropped to the street there was a length of tubular railing, waist-high to an adult. You could go and lean over it. And if you did, you would look down on the neon sign, which was fixed to the wall of the building just below you.

The sign consisted of the two huge letters, A.A. Each letter was about eight feet wide and ten feet deep. Even the tops of the As were fully two feet wide. The letters were totally enclosed by a grey casing at the tops and sides. The fronts, facing away from the building, were of a translucent material, to let the light through.

Down from the roof, where there was a gap in the railing, went a little flight of a dozen narrow metal steps. This too was railed for safety. The steps led to a narrow catwalk that ran along the foot of the giant

letters. The catwalk was railed on the outer side only. A man could stand on it while working on the sign.

But the rail along the catwalk was meant to protect men, not children. To Donald it was at head height.

He was out there on the walkway, gripping the rail with both hands. Below his head level there was nothing between him and space, nothing to save him from the two-hundred-foot drop to the street below.

And Donald's mood had changed again. He wasn't a daredevil now. He was sobbing with fear.

'Kathy!' he called when, hesitantly, she went to the railed edge of the roof and looked down at him. 'Kathy, I don't like it out here. I'm scared!'

Chapter Eight

Mr Hurst was standing beside Kathy.

'Well, come back, then,' he called to Donald. 'And be quick about it.'

But Donald didn't move.

'I won't touch you,' Mr Hurst assured him.

'I don't think he *can* come back,' Mr Swanson said quietly. 'He's terrified. Somebody will have to fetch him.'

Mr Hurst looked uneasy.

'Better not be me, sir, had it?' he said. His usually-loud voice was suddenly subdued. 'I mean ... Well, I seem to put the fear of God into him. There's no telling what he might do if I went out there. He might panic, and then ... Well, I wouldn't like to be the cause of a tragedy.'

And Kathy could see in Mr Hurst's eyes that he was afraid.

'There's no denying I'm not so good at heights,' he went on. 'And it wouldn't help the boy if anything happened to *me*, would it?'

'No, Hurst, it wouldn't,' Mr Swanson said. There

was something in his tone of voice that suggested he didn't think much of Mr Hurst. 'You'd better not try, had you?'

Then Mr Swanson seemed to make up his mind. 'Go and ring the fire brigade,' he told Mr Hurst crisply. 'Use the phone in the Suite. An emergency call. Tell them exactly where the boy is. In the meantime, find one or two able-bodied men who aren't afraid. And a rope. And get them here quickly, man. Quick as you can!'

'Yes, sir,' Mr Hurst said. He disappeared promptly, as if glad to get away from the scene.

Mr Swanson leaned over the railing.

'Donald,' he said. 'I want you to stay where you are until somebody comes to help. Hold on tightly and don't look down.'

Donald's face was white and tear-stained.

'I'm dizzy,' he whimpered. 'I'm going to fall.'

'I'd better go out to him myself,' Mr Swanson said to Kathy. 'If I can just hold his hand to reassure him, it may make all the difference.'

But as he was speaking the crispness went out of Mr Swanson's voice. His face was a whitish yellow. And before he could get to the gap in the railing he seemed to give way at the knees. He clutched at the rail to hold himself up.

'I'll be all right in a minute,' he said faintly. 'There's nothing wrong with *my* head for heights. It's just that I'm a bit feeble. An incident like this takes it out of

me. It's a nuisance being old and decrepit, Kathy. I don't recommend it.'

Donald was crying noisily now.

'I'm coming soon!' Mr Swanson called to him.

But Mr Swanson looked ill as well as frail. He obviously wasn't fit to go out on a catwalk, or indeed to go anywhere at all.

Kathy turned from him and looked over the railing again. Donald caught her eye.

'Kathy!' he wailed. 'Kathy, come! Come quickly, Kathy, I'm still dizzy. I'm going to fall, Kathy, I'm going to fall!'

'I'll go to him,' said Kathy.

'No!' said Mr Swanson. 'No, you mustn't. Let me...'

He tried again to move. And as soon as he let go of the railing he folded gently to the ground.

'Coming, Donald!' Kathy called. 'I'm coming. Now!'

Chapter Nine

'It isn't really happening,' Kathy told herself. 'It *can't* be happening, it must be a dream. If I fell, I'd wake up in bed.'

But she knew it *was* happening. Her hand on the metal rail was damp with sweat. The wind came in gusts, as if trying again and again to prise her hand away from the railing or her feet from the narrow metal steps she had to descend. And Mr Hurst's head for heights couldn't be worse than hers.

Kathy wished she was brave.

She knew it was best not to look down. But she had to see where she was going. She shot a rapid glance at steps, walkway and sign, trying to concentrate on these things that were close to her, and not let her gaze go swooping down the terrifying distance that lay below. But she couldn't avoid it entirely, and for an instant her head swam. She bit her lip and concentrated hard, telling herself she was going to stay in control. And then she was all right again. Just.

There were a dozen metal steps down to the walkway. Holding her breath, Kathy took the first step with her left foot, and brought the right one down to join it. Then she stood trembling, feeling already that she had left safety behind her.

'Come on, Kathy. Hurry!' Donald appealed to her.

Suddenly Kathy felt she had to take the remaining steps at a run or she'd never take them at all. She went down them as if hurrying downstairs at home. And she slipped on the last step. Her wet hand left the rail and she slid into a sitting position. She was on the walkway, and there wasn't much width to it. The bottom step was pressing painfully into her back. Her feet were out in mid-air. All around her was space.

Kathy's legs felt as if they were made of butter. At first she didn't think she could get up at all. There was nothing to hold on to while she did so. Then she wiped her hands on her jeans, pressed her palms flat down on the walkway, and hoisted her bottom on to the lowest step. Then up another step. Then she could get her hand to the rail. She rose, swaying slightly, and was standing on the walkway, her body shaken a little but otherwise none the worse.

Donald hadn't moved. He wasn't looking at Kathy now. He clung to the railing with his head pressed against it. He was sobbing 'Kathy! Kathy!' in a muffled way. There was a damp patch on the front of his shorts where he'd wet himself.

Again Kathy felt the impulse to move rapidly, to run along the walkway towards him, to get it over. But this time she resisted the urge. Her shoe soles were

smooth, she'd slipped once already, she couldn't risk slipping again.

Step by tiny step, she edged along. And then suddenly Donald took his face from the railing, ran to her, and flung his arms round her middle.

'Kathy!' he sobbed again. 'Kathy!' He wasn't holding the rail at all, he was only holding *her*. And the weight of him made her feel off-balance.

With her left hand she gripped the rail as firmly as she could, though the hand was damp with sweat again by now. She put her right arm round Donald's shoulders trying to hold him still. He was the one who was trembling now.

'There, there,' she said. 'It's all right. You *were* a silly boy, weren't you?'

Donald had nothing to say, but clung more tightly.

'Get a hand on the rail, Donald,' she said. 'You're quite safe. I'm holding you.'

He didn't seem to want to take either hand away from her.

'Go on,' she said. 'You'll be more comfortable like that.'

Reluctantly Donald took a hand from her waist and put it on the rail. They stood facing each other in mid-air, each with a hand on the rail and an arm round the other. A gust of wind riffled Donald's hair. Kathy's was stuck to her moist forehead.

She realized she was cold. They were in the shadow cast by the highest part of the building. She had sweated a lot, and now her body was clammy.

She tried to smile. 'There,' she said, 'we're doing fine, aren't we? Shall we try to get back on the roof?'

But Donald shook his head violently.

'Well, never mind,' she said. 'I think the firemen are coming. They'll be here soon, I expect.'

'It's a long way down, isn't it?' said Donald. He shuddered. 'I didn't realize. It didn't feel the same when I was on the roof. It felt all right then.'

There was a fresh gust of wind. Kathy wasn't sure whether the walkway shifted in it, or whether it was her imagination working too hard, as usual.

'I expect they'll spread a net out below,' she said.

'Then somebody'll come out to us. They might put ropes round us, just to make sure.'

Donald clutched her more tightly still.

'I wonder if the fire engine will come,' she said. 'If it does, I suppose we'll see it from here.'

And then, without meaning to, she found herself looking down, down, down to the street, where cars wove in and out. They made a moving pattern of brightly-coloured beetles, far far below.

The walls of the building beside her began to tilt. She closed her eyes, but that was no good. It was as if waves, blood-coloured waves, were rising around her, rising so that she'd drown.

She opened her eyes and looked into Donald's frightened face. That brought her round for the moment.

'Are you still all right?' she asked him.

He nodded. He had stopped sobbing. Perhaps he could feel that she was in difficulty. She bent over and kissed his forehead. Usually Donald hated to be kissed, except by Mum, but this time he liked it, and shifted his hand along the rail to touch hers.

Then a hum began in her head. It was just a little hum at first, like a radio set switched on but not tuned. But it grew louder, more highly pitched, more piercing, until it hurt.

And she wanted to let go. She *wanted* to let go. Only letting go would stop it.

She was swaying. But to her it felt as if the building near by was rocking. Rocking, rocking. Rearing up and diving down. If it went right over on its head, she'd know she'd fallen.

'Kathy!' Donald shouted at her in terror. And the shout stopped the noise in her head, stopped the rocking.

He was staring up into her face with great wide eyes. She smiled, trying to reassure him.

'There's nothing the matter, Donald,' she said. 'We only have to hold on. It's quite easy, isn't it?' And she put her free arm more firmly round his shoulders.

But the rocking was starting again, slight at first, then getting more. And the hum came with it, rising slowly, going up and up until it was past actual sound and she couldn't hear it any more but it was still hurting her head.

She wasn't going to close her eyes again. She wouldn't, wouldn't, wouldn't close her eyes. Yet keeping them open didn't do any good. Nothing would stand still. The handrail, the enormous letters of the neon sign, Donald's head, the rows of windows, the endlessly high walls, the street below, and the pattern of little bright beetle cars – all were swinging and wheeling around her. And up through them all, the blood-red waves were rising. She couldn't tell her surroundings from the waves. The waves were nearly up to her head . . .

'All right, Kathy dear, all right, all right.'

A warm, reassuring voice. The sound of a descent, awkward but determined, down the metal steps. A limping yet steady advance along the walkway. A wide, cheerful smile. An arm placed firmly round her. Dad.

The waves could rise now if they wanted. The waves could wash right over. The waves could flood into her and it wouldn't matter. But they didn't want to, now that Dad was here.

She looked around her, and everything was standing still. Everything was in its place, planted, steady. Everything was all right.

'We'll soon get you out of here,' said Dad.

'I'm not scared,' said Donald. 'I'm not scared at all. Well, not *very* scared.'

Chapter Ten

Nobody knew quite how Dad did it. He'd just got back from the hospital when Mr Hurst came down looking for help. And a man with two good legs could hardly have moved faster. Dad had reached the roof, limped out on to the walkway, got an arm round each child, and brought them safely back, before anyone else was on the spot.

Mr Jones arrived two minutes later, and the firemen a minute or two after that. Their officer was nice about it. He wasn't annoyed that they'd been called out and not needed. So long as the call was genuine, he said, he'd much rather have that happen than not be called when they *were* needed. Personally he wouldn't have advised Dad, with his disability, to go out on the walkway, but there, all was well that ended well. No doubt someone would give Donald a good talking-to when he'd had time to recover. And he hoped that whoever left that ladder from the roof garden to the main roof in place would get a kick in the pants.

He seemed more worried about Mr Swanson than anything else. Mr Swanson had passed right out, and

might have hit his head as he fell. But the President came round as the fireman was leaning over him, and before long was being rather testy with everybody and declaring impatiently that he'd be all right in a minute or two. He didn't look very pleased to see Mr Hurst come pounding up with a coil of rope when the emergency was all over. He was even less pleased to have Mr Hurst and Mr Jones help him down two ladders and across the garden to the Executive Suite. But he listened with interest to the story of how Dad had brought the children in.

Kathy heard most of what went on, but it was as if from a long way away. What she was most conscious of was Dad's arms still round her. When she heard the fireman praise Dad's bravery she felt wonderfully good, and snuggled warmly against Dad's jacket.

Then Donald spoke up.

'Kathy's brave, too,' he said. 'She just can't *stand* heights. Kathy was ever so brave.'

When Mum arrived at Top of the World, the fire officer had gone. Mum made coffee for the other four grown-ups and hot chocolate for Donald. Kathy didn't want anything. Her stomach felt as if it was tied up in knots.

Though Mum didn't show it, Kathy thought she was the most shaken of all. Mum would have gone out on the walkway as readily as Dad, Mum would have gone *anywhere* for them, but she'd been away when it all happened. While the others were drinking their coffee, Mum went quietly out to take the washing off the line, and Kathy, helping her, noticed that her hands were trembling.

'It is just an hour,' Mr Swanson was saying in that thin, precise voice of his, 'since I arrived here to find a child playing in the fountain. And with the exception of an incident in the war, which I won't bore you with, I think it's been the most terrifying hour of my life.'

'It wouldn't do the company any good to have kids falling off the roof, would it?' said Mr Jones cheerfully.

Nobody seemed amused by that remark.

'It appears to me, sir,' said Mr Hurst ponderously, 'that this building is not suitable for children.' Mr Hurst had recovered his confidence by now. He went on: 'Something like this was bound to happen sooner or later. I've told the Staff Manager so. In fact, sir, if I may say so, I'm surprised that a man with a young family was ever given this job.'

'This won't happen again,' said Dad uneasily. 'I can promise you that. They won't get anywhere near the roof from now on.'

'I won't even let them come up here when I'm cleaning,' said Mum. 'And I'm sorry about the washing. This really is the only place to hang washing out. I didn't know anyone was coming to Top of the World today.'

'That's all right,' Mr Swanson said with a touch of

impatience. 'There are more important things to worry about than a line of washing. But...'

He looked at them thoughtfully.

'Do *you* think it's a suitable place for children?' he asked.

Mum said slowly: 'It wouldn't be easy for Dad to get another job. Not with his leg. And a job like this, where we can both of us work and have the children with us – well, until today I've thought of it as a blessing.'

Dad didn't say anything. But Mr Jones butted in, in his usual tactless way.

'Not much fun for the kids, though, is it?' he said. 'Kids need friends their own age. Nobody comes here to play.'

Mum and Dad looked at him appealingly, as if begging him to shut up. But Mr Hurst said with satisfaction, 'Just what I've always thought. The children would be better off living somewhere else.'

'Where?' asked Mum bitterly.

Mr Swanson spoke in the quiet voice that always seemed to silence everybody.

'I've been wondering about two things,' he said. 'First, about the little patch of ground to the right of the back entrance.'

'What patch of ground?' asked Mr Hurst; and then, 'You don't mean the Management Car Park?'

'That's exactly what I mean,' said Mr Swanson. 'Do we really have to have a Management Car Park? Isn't there room for management cars in the main parking area?'

'The best spaces would be taken every day before the management people arrived,' said Mr Hurst doubtfully.

'I imagine there are answers to *that* problem,' Mr Swanson said drily. 'They could try arriving earlier, for instance. Think about it, Hurst. That area is right beside the building, and it's enclosed on three sides already. It seems to me that with very little work it could be made safe for children.'

'It wouldn't look very good, sir,' Mr Hurst objected, 'to have children playing around.'

'Oh, I don't know,' said Mr Swanson. 'For myself, I'd as soon look at children as at cars.' His eye fell on Donald. 'From a safe distance, of course,' he added.

Mr Jones grinned broadly.

'The other thing I've been wondering about,' Mr Swanson went on, 'is why no other children come to the Barretts'. Is it *only* because they can't play out of doors?'

Mum and Dad hesitated. It was Mr Jones who jumped in promptly with the answer. 'Hursty won't have other kids in the building,' he said.

Mr Swanson didn't say anything. He just looked at Mr Hurst, whose face grew gradually redder.

'I have always supposed,' Mr Hurst said at last, 'that this was a serious place of business, not a kindergarten.'

'Quite so, Hurst,' Mr Swanson said. 'I'm glad you show such concern for the company's interests. However ...' He paused, then added with sudden energy, 'For heaven's sake, man, have a heart!'

There was a brief silence. Then Mr Swanson went on, more quietly, 'I suggest you think again about that, Hurst. As for the Management Car Park I'll look into the matter myself. I expect we can make a change quite soon. In the meantime, I don't really mind the children being in Top of the World if they're with an adult. But there mustn't be any more incidents like today's.'

'Or any more washing hung out?' asked Mum with a faint smile.

'I don't object to the washing,' said Mr Swanson. 'I rather like it, in fact. It makes the place more homely.'

Then he turned to Mr Hurst.

'I expect you and Jones have duties to attend to,' he

said. 'And so have I. My luncheon guest will be arriving in' – he looked at his watch – 'good heavens, about twenty minutes!'

'Yes, sir,' said Mr Hurst. He clicked his heels together. 'Mr Jones, attention!' Mr Hurst gave Mr Swanson a smart salute. Mr Jones, as before, stood to attention in a sloppy, embarrassed way.

Donald felt he'd been out of the act too long. And he'd seen enough films to know what came next.

'Stand a-a-at EASE!' he told them both.

Mr Hurst glared. Mr Jones tried not to laugh. Mr Swanson smiled slightly.

'You can take that instruction as final, Hurst,' he said. 'I've had enough of this saluting nonsense.'

But Mum was not amused at all. She grabbed Donald by the arm.

'If I have any more trouble with *you*,' she said, 'you'll get the walloping you deserve!'

'Kathy doesn't want to go to heaven any more,' said Donald that afternoon. The Barretts were back in their own flat. Donald hadn't been walloped, but he'd had the biggest talking-to of his life. And a bit of reaction to the morning's events had set in. Kathy was suffering slightly from shock, and had been tucked up in bed with an out-of-season hot water bottle.

'I'm not surprised she doesn't want to go up there again,' said Mum. 'Though she may change her mind later. As for you, my lad, you won't go to the roof

garden any more unless you're holding a grown-up's hand every minute of the time.'

'I don't want to go there again, either,' said Donald. 'Not just yet, anyway. I don't think I like heaven, after all.' He added thoughtfully: 'Of course, it isn't heaven *really*. It's only Top of the World. I haven't gone to real heaven yet.'

'You nearly did this morning,' said Dad.

About the Author

John Rowe Townsend was born in Leeds, England, and was educated at Leeds Grammar School and at Cambridge University, where he took an honours degree in English and edited the undergraduate newspaper. After working as a journalist on the *Yorkshire Post* and the *Evening Standard*, he joined what was then the *Manchester Guardian* in 1949. From 1955 to 1969 he was editor of the *Guardian*'s weekly international edition, but gave it up in order to have more time for writing.

Mr Townsend has had a lifelong interest in children's books, and in addition to reviewing them in the *Guardian* and elsewhere, he has lectured on books for children in this country and in the United States, and is the author of two studies of children's literature, *Written for Children* and *A Sense of Story*.

An active interest in social conditions surrounding poor children led to his first book, *Gumble's Yard*. His other novels include *The Intruder* (Honours list, Carnegie Medal, 1969; Silver P.E.N. Award, 1970; Boston Globe/Horn Book Award, 1970), *Goodnight, Prof, Love* and *The Summer People*. He is also the author of *Forest of the Night*, a strange, haunting fantasy inspired by Blake's poem *The Tyger*.

We hope you have enjoyed this book. There are 1,000 other Puffins to choose from, and some of them are described on the following pages.

Minnow on the Say

Philippa Pearce

The floods brought the canoe to the foot of David's garden, and the canoe brought David to Adam Codling, its proper owner. That was how David and Adam became friends, scraped and varnished the boat, and named her *Minnow*. Then they made plans for how they should use her.

Of course, they could just paddle her up and down the river, the Say, and picnic and climb the willows and fish, but Adam wanted to do more than that – he intended to use the *Minnow* to find the family treasure which his ancestor had hidden centuries before. Time was running out and with the family in such financial trouble there was little chance that Adam would be there next summer to paddle the *Minnow* on the Say.

Me and My Million

Clive King

Delivering a laundry bag to a launderette *seemed* simple enough. But it meant catching a bus, and Ringo wasn't too strong on reading words and figures. He was quite likely to get a number 41 muddled with 14 – and that was how he came to find himself in the wrong launderette, late at night, with a million pounds' worth of laundry and only 2p in his pocket. It was the start of a series of wild adventures, which were to lead through a derelict fire station, a rich businessman's office, the hideout of a mysterious gang, and a narrowboat on the Regent's Park Canal, in London.

Storm Surge

David Rees

No one was prepared when the water came surging through the walls that night, covering the bridge that joined Flatsea to the mainland and swamping the coastline too. Young Peter Brown was helplessly trapped in his family's pub, where the flood had burst open the doors and was rising steadily up the stairs, and he was worrying desperately about what had happened to his brother Aaron, due back on the last train home after a night out in Ozzedam, or to Martin, who lived on the mainland and had left with his girl friend only a short time ago, or his parents, who had driven into town to see their first grandchild, or to his grandparents alone in their cottage a little way inland.

David Rees tells his story of the flood and its aftermath with great power and clarity. You'll find yourself getting involved with every member of the close-knit family as they face this crisis whose shocking effect is, for more than one of them, a turning point in their lives.

X Marks the Spot

Joan de Hamel

'X marks the spot,' said Cop, but he was too badly injured in the helicopter crash to tell Peter, Louise and Ron more than this. So they had to find it themselves, which wasn't very easy for they not only didn't know what X was, but they had crashed in the middle of the New Zealand bush, with no maps and very little equipment, as most of that had been lost in the river. Making their way through the forest, living off the land, was not the only problem, though, for other people were after the mysterious X, and the helicopter had crashed because it had been sabotaged . . .

Tiger in the Bush

Nan Chauncy

The Lorenny family lived in a secret valley, hidden so deep in the mountains that no map markers had discovered it, where the rarest creatures lived safe from the menaces of hunters or the curiosity of scientists. When Dad and the others were away on a prospecting trip, and Badge and his mother were left in charge of the farm, two friendly strangers appeared and asked to set up camp, and, fatally warming to their friendship and interest, Badge confided to them that the rarest animal of all, the nearly extinct Tasmanian tiger, could still be seen in the valley. The moment he had spoken, he sensed the disaster and, desperate to find a way to undo the damage before the wild and splendid creature was outlawed or killed by too much interest, he embarked on the only plan he could think of, one that was to lead him into real danger . . .

Terry on the Fence

Bernard Ashley

'I'm clearing off. No one wants me in this house. All you do is just shout at me and treat me like a baby. So I'm going off for good!' yelled Terry, and he slammed the front door and set off for the common.

But things didn't work out the way Terry planned. First of all he found his hideout was in ruins, and then the deserted bandstand wasn't deserted after all. Instead, five hostile faces were staring at him, grinning dangerously.

This is a very human story, about an ordinary boy caught up in a web of ugliness and dishonesty, suitable for people of nine or more who enjoy an adventurous read.

Heard about the Puffin Club?

... it's a way of finding out more about Puffin books and authors, of winning prizes (in competitions), sharing jokes, a secret code, and perhaps seeing your name in print! When you join you get a copy of our magazine, *Puffin Post*, sent to you four times a year, a badge and a membership book.
For details of subscription and an application form, send a stamped addressed envelope to:

The Puffin Club Dept A
Penguin Books Limited
Bath Road
Harmondsworth
Middlesex UB7 ODA

and if you live in Australia, please write to:

The Australian Puffin Club
Penguin Books Australia Limited
P.O. Box 257
Ringwood
Victoria 3134